THE BEACH HOUSE

THE BEACH HOUSE

LYNN MARIE GRAY

CREATOR OF BIJOUXS LITTLE JEWELS FROM THE KITCHEN

PHOTOGRAPHY BY LYNN MARIE GRAY

For Andrew
You are the light of my life-the most precious little jewel.

INTRODUCTION	07
RECIPE INDEX	09
THE PICNIC BASKET	11
WAKE UP CALL	19
FROM THE WATER	27
SURF'S UP	43
SWEET DREAMS	51

WELCOME TO THE
BEACH HOUSE

Come in and relax, and don't mind the sand. Whether for a short weekend or a week, the beach house is a place where family and friends gather to truly relax. The Beach House recipe collection evokes memories of restful days spent along the beautiful California shore. Simple food, prepared in a most casual setting, gathered from local seafood markets and vacation village vendors. More than a place, the Beach House recipe collection is a really a state of mind. Casual and convivial, these recipes transport us to warm, restful days and relaxing nights. Listen carefully, you can almost hear the waves.

SANTA BARBARA MUSSELS WITH PERNOD »

FROM THE BEACH HOUSE

WELCOME TO CHANGE, again. Every year since beginning Bijouxs a fresh start has been required and that was never more true than this year. Finally, a new cookbook is here, years in the making. My idea for the cookbooks has stayed true, a modern, portable recipe collection. Simple beautiful food from home, this year it's from The Beach House.

Bijouxs has always been about sharing the little jewels, culinary gems garnered from years of collecting. Style and all its dimensions are also a part of the Bijouxs experience, the visual admiration of the everyday beauty all around us in our kitchens.

The Little Jewels Collection seeks to embody the art and practice of the home cook, reflecting charm, beauty and joy. Bijouxs highlights these simple virtues, and aspires to deliver recipes in a manner that also mirrors the times we live in, including a return to home, hearth and family—when the best table in town is your own.

Change again. Yes, I have welcomed change. I did not set out to create a food blog. More than 10 years ago I began writing and designing what I envisioned as a series of "little jewel" cookbooks. It was a spare time project. I wanted to share the gems of my culinary collection from my years working in and around food. Of course, given the fact that I am also a designer by trade, I would aspire for the cookbook collection to be beautiful, practical, and visually reflect the everyday beauty of cooking at home. In short, beautiful food by design.

Enter some changes of epic proportion. Bijouxs got put on hold. Seeing the wave of change about to crash on my shore, I embraced and found comfort in Bijouxs, a natural evolution of my talents—food and design—and set forth into unknown waters.

Remaining true to oneself feels a bit like being a renegade, and it takes courage to bring forth a creative project for which the only resource is *yourself*. That's how Bijouxs and the Little Jewels Collection began, but with friends' support, trial and error, discipline and a whole lot of work, I am pleased to present, in a decidedly modern format, No. 3 The Beach House.

The irony is that I now live at the beach. My light hair and casual life depict the change. The recipes in this cookbook are ones I cooked for years in rental beaches houses. I want to share them with you.

This is the third of a series of cookbooks, more recipes and more everyday beauty for those of us who cook at home. It goes without saying that I have created The Beach House recipes to please you.

I sincerely hope they will.

LYNN MARIE GRAY

RECIPE INDEX

PICKLED SHRIMP

SUMMER CORN SALAD

MARKET BASKET SALAD

LEMON CRISPS

WAKE UP CALL

CREMESICLE MUESLI

CHOCOLATE CHERRY GRANOLA

RASPBERRY DUTCH BABY

BAKED CHEESE GRITS

FROM THE WATER

BAKED CLAMS DIABLO

BIJOUXS BEST CLAM CHOWDER

SANTA BARBARA MUSSELS

FAMILY-STYLE FILET OF SOLE

RECIPE INDEX

More FROM THE WATER

CURREID SHRIMP SOUP

CALIFORNIA FISH FAJITAS

SEAFOOD IN SAFFRON BROTH

BAKED FISH WITH ALMONDS

SURF'S UP

CAULIFLOWER & AVOCADO RISOTTO

WALDEN SURF OATMEAL COOKIES

SURFER BARS

FRUIT & HONEY

SWEET DREAMS

LAZY BROWNIES

WABI SABI MISO & FRUIT COOKIES

MOM'S INSTANT CHOCOLATE SAUCE

SCALLOPED PINEAPPLE

THE PICNIC BASKET

PICKLED SHRIMP

RECIPE CARD

PICKLED SHRIMP

A SUMMER STANDARD RECIPE THAT TRAVELS BEACHSIDE PACKED IN HUMBLE MASON JARS. ALWAYS A PICNIC FAVORITE, RARELY ARE THERE LEFTOVERS. DOUBLE OR TRIPLE THE RECIPE AS REQUIRED. SERVES 4-6 AS AN APPETIZER

INGREDIENTS

1 pound shrimp, cooked and peeled, tails on
½ medium white onion, sliced into razor thin rings
1 lemon, sliced very thin

For the marinade:
¾ cup safflower oil
½ cup apple cider vinegar
1½ teaspoons celery seed
6 whole black peppercorns
1½ teaspoons kosher salt
1½ teaspoons raw sugar
3 dried bay leaves
Dash of Old Bay Seasoning (optional)

DIRECTIONS

Mix all the marinade ingredients together in a large bowl, stir well to completely dissolve the sugar and salt.

In a 1 quart wide-mouth Mason jar, place a layer of shrimp, then the onion and lemon, repeating the layers until the jar is full, leaving about ¼ inch of headroom.

Pour the marinade over the shrimp and fill to cover the ingredients. Seal the jar tightly. Tilt the jar a couple times side to side to ensure all the shrimp are thoroughly covered by the marinade.

Refrigerate 8 hours, or overnight. Serve with crackers as an appetizer or fill avocado halves with the shrimp, serve with tomato wedges and lettuce for lunch or light supper.

COOK'S NOTES: An inexpensive handheld mandoline style slicer makes quick work of the task of slicing both the onion and lemon into razor thin slices.

SUMMER CORN SALAD

RECIPE CARD

SUMMER CORN SALAD

FRESH, SWEET CORN, LITTLE JEWELS OFF THE COB, PERFECT FOR A SUMMER SALAD. SUMMER CORN SALAD IS COOL, SWEET, CRISP AND CREAMY WITH A TANGY HERB INFUSED DRESSING–A GREAT FLAVOR BURST WHEN PAIRED WITH SEAFOOD. SERVES 4

INGREDIENTS

4 ears fresh sweet corn, cut off the cob

½ small red onion, finely minced

1 avocado, diced

1 red bell pepper, 1/2 diced, 1/2 sliced thin

For the dressing:

1/3 cup olive oil

5 tablespoons red wine vinegar

1 clove garlic, chopped

1 bunch fresh cilantro (tops only), reserve some leaves for garnish

1 teaspoon fresh or 1/2 teaspoon dried oregano

½ teaspoon cumin powder

½ teaspoon mild chili powder

2 dashes Tabasco sauce

Pinch salt

DIRECTIONS

Place all of the dressing ingredients into a blender and blend on high for about 30 seconds until the dressing is smooth. (You may need to scrape down the sides of the blender and blend again to incorporate all the ingredients.)

Place the corn kernels, red onion, avocado and diced red pepper in a bowl and pour on the dressing, toss lightly, cover and chill in the refrigerator 1-2 hours.

To serve, remove the bowl from the refrigerator, toss the salad lightly and pour onto a platter. Garnish with reserved cilantro leaves and red pepper slices.

MARKET BASKET SALAD

MARKET BASKET SALAD

SUMMER SIMPLE=SALADS. WHAT BETTER WAY TO TAKE ADVANTAGE OF THE SEASONAL BOUNTY THAN BY PAIRING SWEET AND SAVORY IN ONE SALAD. A SALAD OF MADE UP OF FARMERS MARKET FINDS THAT HIGHLIGHTS RADICCHIO, FIGS, PEACHES, AND FETA CHEESE, SEASONAL EVERYDAY BEAUTY IN THE KITCHEN, ALWAYS A LITTLE JEWEL. SERVES 4

DIRECTIONS

Prepare the dressing. Whisk together the vinegar, mustard, honey, and slowly drizzle in the oil and continue wisking until dressing is smooth. Taste and season with salt and pepper.

Prepare the *mise en place* to assemble the salad. Start with the radicchio by slicing the root end, and removing leaves, then tearing each leaf in half down the middle ridge of leaf. Slice the figs in quarters. Slice the peaches in half, removing the stone, and slice each half into 1 inch wedges. Cube the feta cheese into 1-inch squares. Last, ready the walnuts, pomegranate seeds, and mint leaves. Items may be prepared 1 hour ahead; store in the refrigerator until ready to serve.

To assemble the salad, begin by laying down some radicchio leaves on the platter. Arrange the figs, peaches, and feta on top. Scatter the pomegranate seeds, walnuts and mint leaves. Drizzle with half the dressing. Serve with extra dressing on the side.

INGREDIENTS

Salad:

1 small head radicchio

4 ripe figs

2 ripe peaches

4 ounces sheep feta cheese

½ cup pomegranate seeds

½ cup toasted walnut halves

1 bunch of fresh mint leaves

Dressing:

¼ white balsamic vinegar

1 teaspoon Dijon mustard

1 teaspoon local organic honey

1/3 cup extra-virgin olive oil

Maldon sea salt & freshly ground black pepper

LEMON CRISPS

LEMON CRISPS

COOKIES ARE ONE OF THE MOST PORTABLE DESSERTS. THESE LEMON CRISPS ARE MADE FROM THE BASICS THAT YOU PROBABLY WILL HAVE ON HAND IN YOUR BEACH HOUSE KITCHEN KIT. PICK UP A FRESH LEMON AND SOME BLANCHED ALMONDS, ALL SUPERMARKET BASICS, AND YOU ARE READY TO BAKE THESE LITTLE CRISPS JUST PERFECT FOR A DAY AT THE BEACH.
MAKES ABOUT 4 DOZEN COOKIES.

INGREDIENTS

1 cup roasted unsalted hazelnuts

Zest of 2 lemons, cut into strips

½ cup salted butter, at room temperature

½ cup sugar

1 egg

1 tablespoon fresh lemon juice

2 teaspoons vanilla bean paste

½ cup sifted all-purpose flour

DIRECTIONS

Preheat oven to 375 degrees. Lightly grease 2 baking sheet pans.

Place the hazelnuts and lemon zest in the bowl of a food processor. Pulse until both are finely chopped.

Put the butter and sugar in a large bowl. Beat with an electric mixer on medium until the butter is light and fluffy, about 3 minutes. Beat in the egg, lemon juice and vanilla bean paste. Add the hazelnut-lemon zest and mix well. Last, add the flour and mix just to combine.

Refrigerate the dough for 30 minutes. Remove from the refrigerator and drop by scant teaspoonfuls onto the baking sheets. Bake for about 10-12 minutes until the edges brown. Allow to cool slightly before removing the cookies.

WAKE UP CALL

CREMESICLE MUESLI

RECIPE CARD

CREMESICLE MUESLI

USUALLY THE FIRST WORDS HEARD IN THE BEACH HOUSE EACH MORNING ARE "WHEN CAN WE GO DOWN TO THE WATER?" TO KEEP BREAKFAST SIMPLE, MAKE IT THE NIGHT BEFORE. THIS NUTRITIOUS BREAKFAST BOWL IS FILLED WITH THE CREAMY FLAVORS OF A COOL OLD-FASHIONED CREMESICLE. MAKES ABOUT 4 CUPS

DIRECTIONS

The night before serving, combine the tangerines, oats, and chopped nuts in a medium sized bowl. Stir in the yogurt, vanilla and juice. Cover and refrigerate overnight. Serve topped with fresh fruit.

COOK'S NOTES: Small oranges can be substituted for the tangerines and also for the juice. Picking up fresh fruit from farm stands on the way to the beach house saves a trip to the market and gives kids a healthy snack for the car ride.

INGREDIENTS

- 4 small tangerines, peeled and segmented
- ¼ cup fresh tangerine juice (from fresh tangerines)
- 1 cup old-fashioned rolled oats
- ¼ cup chopped hazelnuts or almonds
- Two 8-ounce containers plain nonfat yogurt
- One 8-ounce container vanilla low-fat yogurt
- 1 teaspoon vanilla extract
- 1 ½ cups fresh berries, seedless grapes, or bananas (vary the fruit by season)

CHOCOLATE CHERRY GRANOLA

RECIPE CARD

CHOCOLATE CHERRY GRANOLA

PACKING IT UP FOR THE BEACH MEANS BRINGING ALONG THIS VERSATILE AND HEALTHY CHOCOLATE GRANOLA. ROASTED HAZELNUTS AND TART DRIED CHERRIES MAKE IT AN AM OR ANYTIME SNACK–A TASTY STAND-IN FOR A SUGARY TREAT.
MAKES ABOUT 4 CUPS

INGREDIENTS

- 1 cup hazelnuts, roasted and roughly chopped
- ½ cup tart dried cherries
- 3 cups old-fashioned rolled oats
- ¼ cup safflower oil or canola oil
- 2 tablespoons cocoa powder
- ¼ teaspoon instant espresso powder
- ¼ teaspoon kosher salt
- ¼ teaspoon vanilla extract
- ½ cup pure maple syrup

DIRECTIONS

Preheat oven to 350 degrees. Combine the hazelnuts, cherries, and oats in a large mixing bowl, toss together.

In a glass measuring cup or medium bowl, combine the oil, cocoa powder, instant espresso powder, salt, vanilla, and maple syrup. Whisk until smooth.

Pour the cocoa mixture over the oats, tossing well to combine. A nonstick silicone baking spatula works well.

Line a half sheet baking pan with parchment paper, pour the granola onto the pan, spreading evenly, gently pressing it down to the bottom of the pan.

Bake for 30 minutes, stirring and pressing it down about every 10 minutes, for even roasting. Remove from the oven undisturbed, allow to cool completely flat before stirring to encourage it to clump and crisp. Store in an airtight jar.

RASPBERRY DUTCH BABY

RECIPE CARD

RASPBERRY DUTCH BABY

CABIN FEVER. CRISP FRESH AIR, TALL GREEN PINES AND A PRISTINE LAKE–THAT'S THE SETTING IN WHICH THIS LITTLE JEWEL RECIPE FIRST ENTERED MY LIFE ABOUT 25 YEARS AGO. BUTTERMILK RASPBERRY DUTCH BABY. RELAX, IT'S A VACATION. SERVES 6

INGREDIENTS

- 1 stick butter
- 1 cup flour
- 1 teaspoon salt
- 1 cup organic buttermilk
- 6 eggs, beaten
- 1 cup frozen raspberries, defrosted and drained
- ½ cup fresh raspberries
- Powdered sugar for serving
- ½ lemon, cut into wedges

DIRECTIONS

Preheat oven to 400 degrees. Melt 1 stick of butter in a 10-inch cast iron skillet on the stove top, until just foaming. Remove from heat.

In a large bowl blend the flour, salt, buttermilk and eggs until smooth. Slowly pour the mixture into the skillet. Add the defrosted raspberries, spreading them throughout the batter.

Bake in oven for 25 minutes, or until puffed and golden brown. Dust with powdered sugar, scatter fresh raspberries on top, and serve with lemon wedges.

COOK'S NOTES: Use organic buttermilk, look for it at Whole Foods or natural foods stores. Read about it in my blog post. The frozen raspberries cook down to a buttery jam, and the fresh raspberries bring tart freshness.

BAKED CHEESE GRITS

BAKED CHEESE GRITS

SO SIMPLE AND SO DELICIOUS. BUTTERY, QUICK, CHEESY CORN GRITS COME TOGETHER IN AN INSTANT. ENJOY THIS CLASSIC SOUTHERN LITTLE JEWEL FROM BIJOUXS. SERVES 6-8

DIRECTIONS

Preheat oven to 400 degrees. Pour grits and cheese into a large bowl. Add 1 stick of butter. Pour boiling water over the cheese, butter and grits, then stir to mix well.

Add a couple of tablespoons of the grits mixture to the beaten eggs and stir. Add the milk to egg mixture, then pour it back into the grits mixture and stir quickly.

Pour into a 9x12 inch casserole dish and bake uncovered for 45 minutes.

COOK'S NOTES: Baking times vary. Keep an eye on it. Take it out when you like the consistency. Baking longer will produce a firmer grits dish, more like spoon bread. Instant grits are in most supermarkets.

INGREDIENTS

- 2 cups boiling water
- 8 one-ounce packets of instant grits
- 2 eggs, beaten
- 2 tablespoons milk
- 1 cup grated sharp cheddar cheese
- 1 stick butter, room temperature
- Red pepper flakes, to taste

FROM THE WATER

BAKED CLAMS DIABLO

RECIPE CARD

BAKED CLAMS DIABLO

THESE SPICY CLAMS ARE A CINCH TO BAKE IN THE OVEN, TOSS IN THE COOKED SPAGHETTI. A ONE-PAN WONDER TO FEED THE FAMILY. SERVES 4-6

INGREDIENTS

40 clams (5 lbs.)

¼ cup extra-virgin olive oil, plus more for drizzling

10 garlic cloves, smashed with the back of a knife

¼ lb. pancetta, small dice

Handful of fresh basil

Red pepper flakes

¼ cup of white wine

2 pints of cherry tomatoes

Lots of fresh ground pepper

1 lb. spaghetti

DIRECTIONS

Preheat oven to 400 degrees. Bring a large pot of salted water to a boil.

Meanwhile, scrub the clams with a stiff brush under cold running water and discard any that are open.

Put a medium roasting pan over two stovetop burners. Add oil, garlic, pancetta, red pepper flakes, cook till pancetta renders. Add the clams, wine, tomatoes, and a good amount of pepper and toss together. Transfer pan into the oven and roast till clams open up. This will take anywhere from 10-30 minutes, depending on the size of the clams. The key is to wait until they open.

While the clams are cooking, drop the pasta into the water for 7 to 8 minutes. Drain.

When clams open, add the cooked pasta into the same roasting pan to soak up all the good juices and intense flavors. Garnish with fresh basil leaves, lots of pepper, and an extra drizzle of extra-virgin olive oil.

Make sure you have some good crusty bread to soak up the juices, too.

COOK'S NOTES: Use whatever variety of local clams you prefer, just adjust the cooking time to make sure the clams open in the oven. I used small Manila clams, but Littlenecks work wonderfully as well.

BIJOUXS BEST CLAM CHOWDER

RECIPE CARD

BIJOUXS BEST CLAM CHOWDER

CLAM CHOWDER HAS HUMBLE ORIGINS AND IS AT ITS BEST WHEN SIMPLE. THIS RECIPE IS MY TAKE ON CLASSIC CLAM CHOWDER. WHAT MAKES IT DIFFERENT AND DELICIOUS IS ITS VERY LIGHT CONSISTENCY, YET THE CHOWDER IS STILL COMPLETELY PACKED WITH FLAVOR.
SERVES 8

INGREDIENTS

- 4 ounces pancetta, chopped
- 2 medium onions, halved and sliced thin
- 4 large Red Rose potatoes, peeled and diced
- 3 cans clams, 2 minced 1 whole, or 3 minced
- 2 bottles clam broth
- 1 quart half-and-half
- 5 dashes Worcestershire sauce (or more to taste)
- Oyster crackers, for serving.
- Chives, minced for serving

DIRECTIONS

Cook pancetta in large pot until crisp. Remove from the pan, set aside. Cook onions in the pancetta fat until soft.

Add diced potatoes, clam broth, clams and pancetta. Bring to boil, reduce heat to low and simmer until the potatoes are soft, about 30-40 minutes.

Cover and keep warm until serving, or cool and reheat.

Just before serving, add enough half-and-half to the warm clam mixture to reach the desired consistency. DO NOT BOIL after adding the half and half, warm gently.

Serve with oyster crackers.

COOK'S NOTES: The clam mixture can be made anytime during the day, then add half-and-half just prior to serving. Salt pork can be used instead of the pancetta. For a thicker chowder, add crushed oyster crackers to thicken.

SANTA BARBARA MUSSELS

RECIPE CARD

SANTA BARBARA MUSSELS

STEAMING THE FRESHEST MUSSELS WITH PERNOD, AN ANISE LIQUEUR, THEN FINISHING WITH CREAM PLUS A COMBINATION OF FINES HERBS, CREATES A MOST LOVELY BOWL. BE SURE TO SERVE WITH LOTS OF CRUSTY BREAD TO SOAK UP THE CREAMY BROTH. SERVES 4-6

INGREDIENTS

- 1 head garlic, roasted
- 2 large shallots, sliced thin
- ½ teaspoon red pepper flakes
- 4 tablespoons olive oil
- 8 ounces dry vermouth
- 16 ounces Pernod
- 4 pounds fresh mussels, scrubbed and beards removed
- 1 cup heavy cream
- 4 tablespoons unsalted butter
- 4 tablespoons fresh parsley, chopped
- 2 tablespoons fresh tarragon, chopped
- 2 tablespoons fresh chives, chopped
- 2 tablespoons fresh chervil, chopped

DIRECTIONS

To roast garlic, slice off top to reveal individual cloves of garlic. Place cut side up on a double sheet of foil, drizzle with teaspoon of olive oil, sprinkle lightly with salt and pepper, seal in foil. Bake for 45 minutes at 375 degrees. Remove from foil and squeeze gently to remove softened cloves of garlic; mash cloves with a fork and reserve.

Place olive oil in large pot over a medium heat. Add sliced shallots and saute until tender, about 2 minutes. Add reserved roasted garlic and red pepper flakes, saute for 1-2 minutes more until fragrant.

Add vermouth and Pernod to the pan and cook over high heat until reduced slightly. Add the cleaned mussels. Toss with the liquid, cover and cook over a high heat for 2-3 minutes, or until the shells open. Using a slotted spoon, remove the mussels and place them aside in a large bowl. (Discard any mussels that did not open).

Add the cream to the pot with the other liquid and simmer over medium high heat until reduced by half. Return the mussels to the pot, add the butter and fresh herbs, toss to combine. Serve mussels and broth in large bowls with hot toasted baguette to soak up the lovely broth.

COOK'S NOTES: Keep mussels in the coldest part of the refrigerator, in the fish market wrapping. Right before serving, soak the mussels in a large bowl of ice water for 20 minutes to remove any grit. Scrub the shells with a stiff vegetable brush, and remove the beards (the bristly material sticking out from one side) by pulling down toward the hinge of the shell and outward.

FAMILY-STYLE FILLET OF SOLE

RECIPE CARD

FAMILY-STYLE FILLET OF SOLE

GATHER ROUND THE TABLE FOR A CLASSIC FISH FRY, FAMILY STYLE. FILLET OF SOLE IS COOKED IN BROWNED BUTTER AND FINISHED WITH LEMON. SIMPLY DELICIOUS AND EASY. SERVES 4

INGREDIENTS

- ½ cup all purpose flour
- 1 pound sole fillets, about 4 fillets
- Kosher salt and freshly ground black pepper
- 1 tablespoon safflower oil or canola oil
- 8 tablespoons unsalted butter (1 stick)
- 4 large lemons, juiced
- Lemon halves (extra for serving)
- 4 tablespoons chopped parsley (passed separately)

DIRECTIONS

Preheat the oven to 200 degrees. Place the flour on a sheet of waxed paper, add the salt and pepper and toss to combine. Rinse the fish and gently pat dry with paper towels. Dredge fish on both sides with flour; shake off excess.

Heat the oil in large (10-12 inch) saute pan over medium heat until hot. Add 2 tablespoons of butter and heat until the foam subsides and it starts to turn a light golden brown. Add the sole fillets (2 at a time) and cook until golden on the bottom, about 2 to 3 minutes. Gently turn fish over, cook an additional 1 to 2 minutes. Carefully place the fillets on an ovenproof platter and keep warm in the oven while you repeat the cooking process for the remaining fillets, adding a tablespoon or two of butter as needed before adding additional fillets. Monitor the heat of the pan, if the butter or the bits in the pan begin to burn, pour off the butter and bits, add 2 tablespoons of butter and continue on with the sauteing process.

After all the fillets have been cooked and placed on the platter, add the lemon juice to the pan (watch out for spattering) and quickly scrape up the brown bits from the pan, (about 15 seconds). Remove from the heat, add additional butter, about 2 tablespoons, stirring to combine the brown butter pan sauce. Taste, and adjust by adding more lemon, butter or salt and pepper as desired. Immediately pour the brown butter sauce, along with the crispy pan bits, over the fish fillets and serve. Serve with additional lemon halves and a bowl of chopped parsley.

CURRIED SHRIMP SOUP

RECIPE CARD

CURRIED SHRIMP SOUP

WEATHER AT THE BEACH CAN CHANGE–FROM SUNNY AND WARM TO COLD AND FOGGY– ALL IN A MOMENT. THANK GOODNESS FOR THIS CREAMY, QUICK SOUP. SERVE IT HOT OR COLD. ADD SOURDOUGH BREAD AND A SIMPLE SALAD FOR LUNCH OR A LIGHT DINNER READY IN MINUTES. SERVES 4

DIRECTIONS

Slice the shrimp into 1-inch pieces, place in a saucepan along with the half-and-half, sherry and curry powder. Cook over medium-low heat for 8 minutes.

Pour the hot soup into a blender and puree until smooth. Serve hot or cold garnished with chives and freshly ground white pepper.

COOK'S NOTES: Do not cook the soup over high heat or boil; simmer gently over medium-low heat to prevent the half-and-half from curdling.

INGREDIENTS

- ½ pound raw shrimp, cleaned and tails removed
- 2 cups half-and-half
- ½ cup dry sherry
- 4 teaspoons curry powder
- 1 tablespoon minced fresh chives
- Freshly ground white pepper

CALIFORNIA FISH FAJITAS

RECIPE CARD

CALIFORNIA FISH FAJITAS

TACOS, I MUST ADMIT THEY ARE PRETTY MUCH A STAPLE IN MY DIET. MY FAVORITE ARE THESE SIMPLE FISH FAJITAS MADE WITH FRESH FISH CAUGHT RIGHT OFF THE COAST OF MY HOME. AN EASY PREP AND DELISH ANY NIGHT OF THE WEEK, FOR MORE THAN JUST TUESDAYS.

SERVES 4-6

INGREDIENTS

- 1-2 California rockfish (snapper) fillets, skin on
- 1-2 tablespoons olive oil
- 1 large onion, peeled, halved and sliced thin
- 1 red and 1 yellow bell pepper, seeded and sliced thin
- Dozen handmade corn tortillas
- Cilantro leaves, chopped
- Salsa of your choice
- Avocado slices

DIRECTIONS

Heat a medium cast iron skillet over an outdoor open grill (beach) or on medium heat on gas stovetop. Add olive oil, heat, add the onion and peppers to the pan, adding more oil if necessary and toss lightly until soft and cooked through, about 5 minutes. Remove onions and peppers from skillet, set aside on a plate.

Place fish skin side down in the skillet adding more oil as necessary. Allow the fish to cook until the skin is crisp and browned, about 5-7 minutes. Carefully turn the fish and brown quickly on the remaining side. Gently lift and remove fish to a plate. Carefully slide a knife or metal spatula under the skin to separate it from the fish.

Return the vegetables and fish to the skillet. Gently flake the fish, tossing with the onions and peppers. Remove the fish and vegetables to a serving plate, cover with foil and keep warm. Warm tortillas for about 1 minute per side; you should see some browning. Remove and wrap with foil to keep warm; repeat with remaining tortillas.

Fill tortillas with fish and vegetables, add cilantro leaves. Avocado and salsa are perfect additions.

COOK'S NOTES: California rockfish, also known as rock cod or Pacific snapper is a fairly common fish on the West Coast. Use snapper or any firm white fish you prefer for the tacos. In fact, just about anything you can wrap in a tortilla—roasted sweet potatoes, or any combination of veggies—makes for a great taco.

SEAFOOD IN SAFFRON BROTH

SEAFOOD IN SAFFRON BROTH

THIS STEAMING BOWL OF GOLDEN BROTH IS A PERFECT SOUP BASE FOR FRESH SEAFOOD FROM A LOCAL FISH MONGER AT THE BEACH HOUSE. ALL YOU NEED TO ADD IS CRUSTY BREAD TO MOP UP THE FLAVORFUL BROTH. SERVES 2 AS MAIN COURSE

INGREDIENTS

- ½ fennel bulb
- 1 medium onion
- 1 large plum tomato
- 1 large garlic clove, smashed
- ½ pound mussels or clams
- ¾ pound large shrimp or crab legs
- ¼ teaspoon crumbled saffron threads
- ½ cup dry white wine
- 1 ½ tablespoons olive oil
- 3 cups fish stock or low-salt chicken broth
- 3 green onions, tops sliced
- Crusty bread

DIRECTIONS

Trim fennel bulbs, discarding stalks. Finely chop fennel and onion. Seed tomato and finely chop. Mince garlic. Scrub mussels/clams well and remove beards. Shell shrimp and devein. Wash and break crab into 3-inch pieces. Stir saffron into wine.

In a 4-quart pan, cook fennel and onion in oil over moderate heat, stirring, until slightly softened, about 5 minutes. Add garlic and cook, stirring, 1 minute. Add wine mixture and simmer until reduced by half, about 3 minutes. Add mussels or clams with 1/2 cup stock and simmer, covered, stirring occasionally, until most mussels/clams are opened, about 2 minutes. Add shrimp or crab legs, tomato, and remaining 2 1/2 cups stock and cook at a bare simmer until seafood is just cooked through, about 2 minutes. (Discard any unopened mussels.) Add the green onions. Season mixture with salt and pepper.

Divide seafood between 2 bowls and ladle broth over it. Garnish seafood with lemon wedges and serve with crusty bread to soak up the sauce.

COOK'S NOTES: The recipe is expandable to feed more, but I usually serve this as a special grownup meal and serve the kids a simple bowl of pasta with butter and cheese. Also, feel free to substitute the seafood combination. I went with what was local and fresh.

BAKED FISH WITH ALMONDS

RECIPE CARD

BAKED FISH WITH ALMONDS

EXOTIC SOUNDING RECIPE BUT ACTUALLY THIS IS A SIMPLE BAKE FOR FRESH WHITE FISH. CRUSTED WITH A SWEET AND SPICED ALMOND CRUST, THE FLAVORS ARE SIMILAR TO CLASSIC BASTILLA. VIA MY TAKE ON A RECIPE BY PAULA WOLFERT IN *COUSCOUS AND OTHER GOOD FOOD FROM MOROCCO.* SERVES 4-6

INGREDIENTS

For the sauce:

- 1 ½ cups unsalted dry toasted slivered almonds
- 1 ½ cups powdered sugar
- 1/3 cup water
- ¼ cup olive oil
- 6 tablespoons unsalted butter, softened
- 1 tablespoon orange juice
- 1 teaspoon ground cinnamon

For the fish:

- 1 large onion, sliced into thin rings
- 4-6 halibut fillets

DIRECTIONS

In a blender or food processor, place almonds, sugar, water, olive oil, orange juice and butter. Blend to make a smooth sauce. Chill for 15 minutes, the sauce will thicken when chilled.

Preheat oven to 400 degrees. Grease a large ovenproof baking dish with butter. Lay the onion slices in the dish to act as a bed for the fish. Add 1/4 cup water to dish. Place the halibut fillets on top of the onion slices. Spread a generous quantity of the chilled almond sauce over the fish.

Bake uncovered about 35-45 minutes until the fish is cooked and the almond sauce is toasty and falling into the onions. Serve with onions, steamed couscous or rice, and drizzle all with pan sauce.

COOK'S NOTES: I was able to attend a Moroccan cooking class taught by Paula as part of my cooking curriculum. Oh I was so young then and it was such an honor.

SURF'S UP

RAW CAULIFLOWER "RISOTTO"

RAW CAULIFLOWER "RISOTTO"

THIS LIGHT SALAD TRAVELS WELL TO THE BEACH. IF YOU ARE MAKING IT AT HOME, USE THE FOOD PROCESSOR TO CHOP HERBS TO MAKE THE CHILI GARLIC DRESSING. SERVES 2-4

DIRECTIONS

In a large bowl dice and smash the avocado. Next, add zest and juice 1 lemon.

Grate or finely chop garlic and chili. Chop the fresh herbs. Add a generous amount of olive oil and mix everything together. You want this to have a loose consistency.

Next, slice florets off the central cauliflower stock and chop fine, until about the size of rice. Add to the lemon mixture.

Mix in the avocado a spoonful at a time until you reach the desired consistency. Serve chilled.

INGREDIENTS

1 avocado

Zest and juice of 1 lemon

1 head cauliflower, chopped fine

1 clove of garlic

1 bunch of mint

1 bunch of cilantro

1 jalapeno chile, seeds removed

A big glug of olive oil

WALDEN SURF COOKIES

RECIPE CARD

WALDEN SURF COOKIES

THESE ARE FAMOUS COOKIES FROM SURFING LEGEND STEVE WALDEN. THEY ARE SO FAMOUS THAT HE HAS AN ONGOING REQUEST TO BRING HUNDREDS OF THEM TO EVERY SURFING CONTEST. MAKES 36 COOKIES

INGREDIENTS

- 2 ½ cups flour
- 4 cups rolled oats
- 2 eggs (or 3 tablespoons of flax meal and 6 tablespoons water or 1/3 cup of pumpkin puree or 1/3 cup applesauce)
- 1 teaspoon baking soda
- 1 teaspoon baking powder
- 1 teaspoon vanilla
- 1 cup white sugar
- 1 cup brown sugar
- 1 teaspoon sea salt
- ¼ cup maple syrup
- 1 ½ cups chocolate chips
- 2 sticks butter, softened

DIRECTIONS

Preheat oven to 350 degrees. Combine the flour and oats in a bowl.

Stir eggs (or wet ingredient substitutes) with sugars, baking powder, baking soda salt and maple syrup. Add chocolate chips and softened butter. Mix well.

Drop by spoonsful on baking sheets lined with parchment paper or silicone baking mat. Bake for 8-12 minutes but do not overbake.

COOK'S NOTES: There are a few egg substitutes listed if you do not eat eggs. The butter should be very soft, at room temperature to easily blend into the batter.

SURFER BARS

RECIPE CARD

SURFER BARS

READY, SET, SURF. THESE BARS ARE A REAL BURST OF ENERGY BEFORE HITTING THE WAVES. MAKES 27 1X3 INCH BARS

INGREDIENTS

- ¼ cup unsalted butter
- ¼ cup organic coconut brown sugar
- 1 cup butterscotch chips
- 1 egg, room temperature and lightly beaten
- 1 teaspoon vanilla bean paste
- ¾ organic unbleached flour
- 1 teaspoon aluminum-free baking soda
- 1 teaspoon kosher salt
- 1 cup dark choclate chips
- 1 cup mini marshmallows

DIRECTIONS

Preheat oven to 350 degrees.

Butter a 9x9 inch baking pan. In a medium saucepan melt the butter over medium heat. When melted, add sugar and stir until sugar dissolves and mixes with the butter. Pour in the butterscotch chips and stir until melted. The chips will not melt completely and the mixture will be grainy.

Transfer mixture to a large mixing bowl, add egg and vanilla, mix well. Add the flour, baking powder and salt, stir to combine. Last, mix in the chocolate chips and marshmallows.

Smooth the mixture into the buttered pan and bake for 20-25 minutes until bars are cooked through.

Cool completely. Remove from pan. Slice the bars into 1x3 inch bars. Wrap in waxed paper and tie with string. Keep the bars cool in the picnic basket.

COOK'S NOTES: These bars are super charged, so one has plenty for power to paddle out into the waves.

FRUIT & HONEY

RECIPE CARD

FRUIT & HONEY

WHAT GOES TOGETHER BETTER THAN FRUIT AND HONEY? THIS SIMPLE, LIGHT FRUIT SALAD FOR THE BEACH IS FLEXIBLE AND SO EASY TO PREPARE. A HEALTHY SWEET FOR SWIMMERS AND LOUNGERS TO SAVOR IN THE WONDERFUL SUNSHINE. USE TOP QUALITY LOCAL ORGANIC HONEY AND FRESH FRUIT FROM THE FARMERS MARKET. SERVES 4-6

INGREDIENTS

- 1 pound mixed sliced fruit, frozen or fresh
- ½ cup fresh raspberries
- ½ cup organic local honey
- ½ cup spring water

DIRECTIONS

Place fruit and fresh raspberries in a large bowl.

Add honey and water to a saucepan and bring to boil on the stove. Pour the hot honey syrup over the fruit. Cover and place in the refrigerator to chill.

When heading out to the beach, place the fruit and syrup in a 4-cup container with a tight-fitting lid. Pack into the beach cooler along with small bowls and bring some long toothpicks to grab your favorite fruit. Serve the fruit with a splash of the honey syrup.

COOK'S NOTES: Mixed sliced frozen fruit works well for this recipe, such as melon, pineapple, mango etc. I like to include one fresh fruit, such as fresh berries, to add a burst of color and flavor.

SWEET DREAMS

LAZY BROWNIES

RECIPE CARD

LAZY BROWNIES

LAZY BROWNIES ARE MADE IN ONE SAUCEPAN, POURED INTO A BAKING PAN AND PRODUCE A THIN, BUT VERY RICH BROWNIE CAPPED WITH SHINY, CRISP CRUST. REQUIREMENTS ARE BASIC KITCHEN STAPLES OF BUTTER, EGGS, SUGAR, VANILLA, FLOUR, AND OF COURSE UNSWEETENED BAKER'S CHOCOLATE, WHICH SHOULD ALWAYS BE LOITERING AROUND THE PANTRY FOR JUST SUCH LAZY BROWNIE MOMENTS. MAKES 16 TWO-INCH BROWNIES

INGREDIENTS

- 8 tablespoons (1 stick) unsalted butter
- 2 ounces unsweetened chocolate, roughly chopped
- 1 cup granulated sugar
- 2 large eggs
- ½ teaspoon vanilla
- ¼ cup all-purpose flour
- Pinch of salt
- ½ cup chopped nuts (optional)
- ½ teaspoon espresso powder (optional)
- Confectioner's sugar for topping (optional)

DIRECTIONS

Preheat the oven to 325 degrees. Butter and flour an 8-inch square baking pan.

In a medium saucepan, melt the butter and chocolate over low heat until both the butter and chocolate are completely melted. Remove from the heat. Stir in the sugar, eggs and vanilla and mix with a wire whisk until the ingredients are thoroughly combined and the sugar is no longer grainy. Stir in the flour and salt. Add chopped nuts or espresso powder if using, and mix again to combine.

Bake the brownies for about for about 40 minutes, or until the batter has set and the crust is crisp and shiny. These are a thin and moist brownie. Allow to cool almost completely before cutting into 2-inch squares. Sprinkle with confectioner's sugar if desired.

COOK'S NOTES: These are simple one-bowl brownies with a few extras such as espresso powder and confectioner's sugar added for good measure.

WABI SABI COOKIES

RECIPE CARD

WABI SABI COOKIES

MAKING THESE COOKIES IS THE EPITOME OF WABI SABI, SIMPLE IN BOTH INGREDIENTS AND APPEARANCE. WABI SABI MISO FRUIT AND NUT COOKIES ARE BARELY SWEET, AND MADE CHEWY WITH FRUIT AND NUTS. A FRIEND DESCRIBED THEM AS ALMOST A FRUIT AND NUT CHEW. THE INCLUSION OF MISO PASTE ADDS A SALTY UMAMI, THE FRUIT PROVIDING A BALANCING SWEETNESS.
MAKES 16 COOKIES

INGREDIENTS

- 1 cup cassava flour
- ½ teaspoon baking powder
- 1/8 teaspoon sea salt
- ¼ teaspoon freshly grated nutmeg
- 1 tablespoon toasted sesame seeds
- 3/8 cup golden monk fruit sweetener
- 3/8 cup avocado oil
- 2 tablespoons light miso paste
- ¼ cup unsweetened vanilla almond milk
- 1 teaspoon vanilla extract
- ¼ cup flaked coconut
- ¼ cup coconut ribbons
- ½ cup dried cranberries
- ½ cup golden raisins
- ¼ cup macadamia nuts, roasted, salted and chopped

DIRECTIONS

Preheat oven to 350 degrees.

Mix the flour, baking powder, salt, nutmeg and sesame seeds. Combine monk fruit sweetener, avocado oil, miso, almond milk and vanilla extract in medium bowl, whisking until smooth.

Add the dry ingredients to the wet and stir until just combined. Fold in the coconut, dried cranberries, raisins, and macadamia nuts.

Chill dough about 15 minutes. Line sheet pan with parchment paper. Roll dough into 2-inch balls and flatten each on the cookie sheet.

Bake for about 15 minutes, until edges brown.

COOK'S NOTES: The cookies have a cracked, imperfect finish, hence the name "wabi sabi" (simplicity, the economy of things and appreciation of the imperfect). These barely sweet cookies are chewy with fruit and nuts, perfect to snack on any time. And they're gluten-free!

INSTANT CHOCOLATE SAUCE

RECIPE CARD

INSTANT CHOCOLATE SAUCE

THIS SAUCE IS ONE OF THE MOST CHOCOLATE-INTENSE SAUCES I HAVE EVER ENCOUNTERED. WE WOULD BEG MY MOM TO MAKE IT TO TOP OUR ICE CREAM. SIMPLE GENIUS. SERVES 4

INGREDIENTS

3 ounces unsweetened Baker's chocolate
½ cup water
2 tablespoons granulated sugar
ice cream for serving

DIRECTIONS

Break the chocolate along the scored lines into 6 pieces. Place the chocolate, water and sugar in a small heavy pan.

Cook over low-medium heat, stirring constantly to melt chocolate and blend sugar. After a few minutes the chocolate will melt and mix into the water.

Continue to stir and cook at a low boil until sauce begins to thicken. The sauce will tighten quickly as the water cooks off. Let the sauce thicken to a hot fudge consistency.

Serve immediately, while still warm, over ice cream. Enjoy quickly, the ice cream will start to melt.

COOK'S NOTES: Adjust the sweetness to suit your taste. I love bittersweet, so I add just a teaspoon or so of sugar.

SCALLOPED PINEAPPLE

RECIPE CARD

SCALLOPED PINEAPPLE

THE BEACH HOUSE IS A PLACE TO UNWIND, WHERE EVERYONE CAN KICK BACK. KEEP IT SIMPLE IN THE KITCHEN WITH THIS CLASSIC SCALLOPED PINEAPPLE-JUST 5 INGREDIENTS, ALL AT THE SUPERMARKET. SERVES 6

INGREDIENTS

- Three 20-ounce cans crushed pineapple, packed in natural juice
- 3 large organic eggs, beaten
- 2 cups organic turbinado sugar
- 1 cup melted salted butter
- 4 cups brioche bread cubes, about 6 slices

DIRECTIONS

Preheat oven to 350 degrees.

Mix together all the ingredients in a large bowl. Pour into a greased round 10-inch baking dish.

Garnish with flaked coconut and serve warm with pineapple sherbet.

COOK'S NOTES: You can use slices of French bread cubes to equal 4 cups.

ABOUT THE AUTHOR

LYNN MARIE GRAY is a food blogger, food photographer and stylist. Lynn is a native of Los Angeles and worked as a personal chef for more than 7 years. Her education and business career focused on retail and graphic design.

After years working in the design world, Lynn founded Bijouxs Little Jewels from the Kitchen in 2010 as a resource for both budding and seasoned cooks. The site's recipes and cooking tips drew followers from around the world. If you love simply beautiful food, I invite you to join me at Bijouxs, that is designed for those of us who cook at home. You will feel welcome here at **BIJOUXS LITTLE JEWELS FROM THE KITCHEN.** You will find easily-prepared, time-tested recipes from my 30 years personal collection.

The Beach House is the third in a series.

LITTLE JEWELS FROM THE KITCHEN
BIJOUXS

THE LITTLE JEWELS COLLECTION

Founder and Creative Director **Lynn Marie Gray**

I offer sincere and profound thanks to my family and friends, who have provided the continuing encouragement that helped make The Beach House possible. Here are a few of the very talented people who so graciously donated their time and expertise to the project. MERCI!

COPY & RESEARCH

Copy Editor **Brian Weiss WORD'SWORTH**

DIGITAL & PHOTOGRAPHY

Digital Production **Dario Di Claudio**

Photography Consulting **William Livingston, Mitchell Haddad**

Portraits **Shannon Cottrell**

4 BEAUTIFUL FOOD BY DESIGN arriving soon...

Bijouxs | Little Jewels Collection - Volume 3 - The Beach House
For advertising, sponsorship, special project or partnership inquires, contact us at info@bijouxs.com.

Copyright © 2020 by Bijouxs.com
All rights reserved. No part of this publication may be reproduced, distributed or transmitteed in any form or by any means without prior written permission of the author. For permission requests, please email info@bijouxs.com.

Lightning Source UK Ltd.
Milton Keynes UK
UKHW051950090820
367868UK00003B/54